Bare, Bold, & Beautiful

Seeking His Light in Every Dark Place

Breyonia Belle

Volume 1

THIS BOOK IS
PUBLISHED BY BREYONIA BELLE

Cover design by Prints Magoncia
Layout design by Manish Pathak

Acknowledgement

I want to first give all the glory and honor to my heavenly Father. Truly this book would not have been written if it were not for Him. The words on these pages were all from Him and none of my own. I will always love you, Jesus, for being loyal, patient, understanding, and faithful to me throughout my journey. I will never forget that you chose me when nobody else would! Thank you so much, Lord. I dedicate my entire being to you in Jesus' name.

I want to thank Christian Culture Entertainment for bringing my vision to life and making a dream come true. Patty Rice, thank you for reaching out to me. I truly believe you were God sent because the way all of this came together is still a blur. Tonja Rice, thank you for making this process so easy and making this book exactly what I envisioned!!

I also want to thank Donnivan, Daylen, and Daxton for your support and motivation. Last but not least, I want to thank my Kingdom Husband Dayne. My love, you spoke life into this book when I felt defeated. When I doubted myself, you reminded me of what God said. Thank you so much, Boopie. I love you all so much!

"Alas, Sovereign Lord," I said, "I do not know how to speak; I am too young." But the Lord said to me, "Do not say, 'I am too young.' You must go to everyone I send you to and say whatever I command you. Do not be afraid of them, for I am with you and will rescue you," declares the Lord. Then the Lord reached out his hand and touched my mouth and said to me, "I have put my words in your mouth. See, today I appoint you over nations and kingdoms to uproot and tear down, to destroy and overthrow, to build and to plant."

- Jeremiah 1:6-10, New International Version

Table of Contents

1

Introduction

A sunflower is a weed that also happens to be a flower. In my opinion, sunflowers are less desirable because it's a type of weed and personally, they are not as pretty as roses, orchids, tulips, carnations or lilacs to name a few. I would never even think of a sunflower as being beautiful until God gave me a dream.

In the dream there was a sunflower in the middle of what looked like a desert. The sky was very cloudy and there was barely any sunlight coming through. What stood out to me was that whenever the beam of sunlight found a way through the clouds, the sunflower would turn in its direction. The sunlight moved a few times, and I was amazed that every single time the sunlight moved, the sunflower found the light.

Because I didn't understand what the dream meant, I googled to see if it was true that sunflowers move with the sun, and from what I saw THEY DO! I learned that young flowers follow the sunlight throughout the day. However, when they mature, the flowers will stop following the sunlight because the initial sunlight they receive is enough to sustain them for the rest of the day. I googled the spiritual meaning of a sunflower and discovered that it symbolizes worship and faithfulness. Google reads that "a sunflower is related to spiritual knowledge and the yearning to seek light and truth." Like a sunflower, I was seeking God's wisdom, revelation, truth, and love. I was worshiping God and praising Him even when I was in a dark and deserted place. Developing this new relationship with Christ, I persistently seek His face throughout the day, every day. And I would like to believe, as a mature Christian, I will be confident to know He is always there even when I don't hear Him.

***

When you begin to gain understanding, you begin to see things differently. What once was undesirable or hopeless can turn out to be something so beautiful, something that God can use. Like the sunflower I once disliked, I now see the beauty in all that I have experienced during my time in the wilderness and the process that got me to this point in life to help others.

On June 30, 2019, I had a dream that I was crying to a friend about my book reaching women all over the world, and them being healed because of the testimonies in my book. In the dream, I was overwhelmed with joy and was so happy to be used by the Lord. I'm proud to say that on June 30,2020, I finally completed my book! Now, let me give you the rundown of how this book came to be . . .

In early 2019, God gave me the desire to start writing this book. I was obedient and started writing, but none of what I wrote made it onto the pages in this book. I had my own idea and vision of how I wanted my first book to be, but God had other plans.

During my wilderness season, which is another way of saying lonely season, I began writing my prayers in a journal. Journaling felt like an urgency to release whatever was on my mind. I get the gratification of releasing all my thoughts and emotions on paper and sending a prayer to God at the same time. One day, God started speaking to me as I journaled. He then continued to speak to me daily during my writing time. I would start to journal to release my thoughts, and would hear God speak, which are actually like thoughts. I know it's Him because of this overwhelming peace and stillness I feel, and the thoughts aren't things I would think of on my own.

God was downloading His wisdom regarding certain situations for which I was seeking His guidance. To make a long story short, in April of 2020, God told me that the journal was my book! I was then instructed to start other projects but on June 24, 2020, God told me to finish my book in seven days. Hearing that made me feel excited and defeated at the same time. I understood that becoming an author was coming to fruition, and I was excited about that, but the unknown of what would happen after the book was released made me want to throw it all away.

Fast forward to June 30,2020. While I was going over one of the chapters, I was "randomly" reminded of another dream I had in 2019. In my dream, there was a group of women who did not want to receive my book. I think they were publishers. They wanted me to change my book to how they wanted it to be written and I wasn't feeling it. I wanted my book to be raw and written the way that God wanted it to be, so I just left.

I went back to my records of dreams but could not find that exact dream. However, as I scrolled through my dreams, God showed me that exactly one year before I had the dream of my book reaching women all over the world. You guys, I cried. That was so amazing to me! I really can't describe how joyful I was! It was confirmation on so many levels. The power of God is real, and this is just the beginning of what I want to share with you.

The words in this book are literally what the Holy Spirit led me to write. When I went back to edit the book, I was ministered to like it was my first time reading it. God is that powerful! God used me to minister to myself and I didn't even know it. The revelations God gave me are still relevant. There were even scriptures highlighted to me that I've incorporated to help those who are like me who want a Biblical reference, and for those new in Christ who may not have a Bible. I truly believe this book is prophetic and I pray that whoever is reading this, God will minister to you through my life experiences. In Jesus' name, Amen!

2

Something Out of Nothing

Before I gave my entire life to God, I did whatever I wanted. I did whatever *felt* good to me, even if it was only temporary. I was constantly trying to fill my life with so many things to feel happy, to feel like I was special, to feel accepted, but what *felt* good never lasted. After all the different things I did to fill myself with, I kept getting the same exact result which was more emptiness. The world's idea of being "happy," "free" or "successful" makes you heavy. We lose our identity of self to be just like the next person. In a constant chase to keep up with the world that leads to absolutely nowhere, we also lose sight in who God really is by replacing Him with idols. We chase material things and people to feel better about ourselves. I believe we do way too much to *feel* wanted and desired but none of it means anything. We spend a lot of energy just to be empty in the end. Do you see how crazy that is?

I smoked weed, had a lot of sex, watched porn, masturbated, and constantly fed my spirit with toxic music. What drove me to consuming the world and everything that gratified the flesh was pain. Underneath my smile, sassy attitude, and witty jokes, I was angry, hurt and never satisfied. I was always secretly in competition with everyone. I gossiped and judged just to feel better about myself. I assumed I had my life under control, but it was the complete opposite. My life was a mess! The truth is I was lost, and I was on the move to find something that made me feel whole. I turned to everything but God when He is the ONLY one that could fill my emptiness.

We are all designed to worship God and Him alone, but when we don't really give Him our hearts, we worship other things. Everything I named earlier was idolatry. An idol is something that takes the place of God. And if you don't know who God is supposed to be to us, He's supposed to be our everything. God wants to be our everything, literally everything you can think of in a loving way though, not like an overbearing boyfriend/ girlfriend. If I use myself for an example, I need God to be my Father, friend, counselor, peace, security and my joy. But instead, I continued to look to everything and everyone BUT God to fill my emptiness. Nothing I did was ever enough, but I promise you, as soon as I surrendered, and I mean AS SOON as I surrendered to Him, the weight I was carrying was lifted. Isn't that ironic? I felt lighter when my emptiness was filled with His greatness.

God takes our everyday burden but that's not all. He takes our shortcomings and makes them beautiful. Have you ever watched the show, *Chopped* on Food Network? Well, if not, it's a show where these chefs have to create an amazing dish out of completely random ingredients in 30 minutes or less. The chefs use food that doesn't complement one another and may not even taste all that great, but these chefs always amaze me at how they can turn something out of nothing. Not just something that is edible, but something that is beautiful to look at and eligible to be served at a 5-star restaurant. These chefs have the ability to transform the taste of undesirable food into something that tastes amazing.

God is our Chopped Chef! We keep giving Him a bunch of random ingredients that do not taste good, look good, smell good and is just hard to work with. We fornicate, we lie, we masturbate, we cheat, we have addictions, we kill, we do perverted things, we steal, we mock, we do drugs, we commit adultery, and more, and yet He has the ability and desire to whip up something amazing out of all that. That's called MINISTRY. When we COMMIT our lives to Him that's when the clock starts and He gets to work. God is a gentleman; He waits for our yes to begin our transformation. He literally makes beauty from ashes!

I openly tell my testimony because I see how much God is transforming my life. I made a choice to receive Jesus as my Lord and Savior, so now I am free from everything I have done in the past. I'm forgiven and healed as far as I can see. I can help others with my testimony by showing people how real God is and how amazing His unchanging love is. It's literally the BEST gift we could ever have.

Are you ready to see what God can transform you into? I promise when you fully commit to God, you will be amazed by the results . . . if you haven't already.

Prayer:

Father God,

I thank You for being such a loving God. Your love for me is literally unfathomable. I am so grateful. God, I ask that You forgive me for all that I have done knowingly and unknowingly. I pray that You forgive me for choosing worthless idols over you. Forgive me for not giving You my whole heart and not committing myself to You. I repent, O God. I ask that you take this burden, O God and give me an appetite for Your Kingdom. Let there be a disgust for the things that aren't of You. Father show me where I am hurting and heal it, Lord. I want to be free in You, O God. Take my sins and wash them away. I ask that You give me a new heart Lord, a pure heart and transform me to the woman/man You have called me to be. Gently guide me Lord and teach me Your ways so that my life will be pleasing to You. I am dedicated to You Lord this day forward.

Thank You for another chance!

In Jesus's Name, Amen.

Scriptures

2 Timothy 2:21-22, NLT
If you keep yourself pure, you will be a special utensil for honorable use. Your life will be clean, and you will be ready for the Master to use you for every good work. Run from anything that stimulates youthful lusts. Instead, pursue righteous living, faithfulness, love, and peace. Enjoy the

companionship of those who call on the Lord with pure hearts.

Proverbs 10:28, NIV
The prospect of the righteous is joy, but the hopes of the wicked come to nothing.

Colossians 3:5, NIV
Put to death, therefore, whatever belongs to your earthly nature: sexual immorality, impurity, lust, evil desires and greed, which is idolatry.

Jonah 2:8, NIV
Those who cling to worthless idols turn away from God's love for them.

3

Do You Know Who You Are?

Jesus didn't argue with people. When people asked Him ridiculous questions or made offensive comments, He remained silent. When demons spoke to Him, He just rebuked them and kept it pushing. How did He do it though? It's easier said than done, well for me at least. I kept finding myself drained after a verbal battle time and time again. I couldn't understand why I could not just shut up! In almost every argument I've had, it would always start off with me thinking I had it under control, and I would just speak my piece in peace. Very seldom was I able to keep a cool head after being lied to or offended. But why? Why was this so hard to do? I believe the difference between me and Jesus in these moments was that Jesus had nothing to prove. He knew who He was and there was no need to defend or explain Himself to His enemies. He knew He was the Son of God. Then it hit me! We have to give up the need to prove ourselves to others. We need to let go of the need to be right, the need for people to agree with us and the need to return an offense.

The root of these needs is because of an identity issue. Needing to be approved, heard, noticed and understood by people isn't what God wants for us. We have to let God be enough for us to be secure in our identity. People are people – meaning they usually get moved based on their emotions. Most people will only see what they want to see or what they are told to see. It's useless to seek approval from anyone other than God. People, or should I say "the flesh," is inconsistent. We can be one way one minute and completely switch up on people based on our circumstances. We don't have it all together. Even our faith can waiver. But one thing about God that I love is that He remains constant and unchanging no matter what. Even in our unfaithfulness, God is faithful and true. It is written in Romans 3:4 that God is true and every man a liar. I don't believe God is trying to offend any of us when He says this. The point is to depend on God's truth.

An example of how inconsistent people are would be having someone, maybe a friend, spouse, or relative, compliment you and then when you let them down, they snap on you. All of a sudden, every compliment was no longer true. Now they want to punish you because of how they feel. Sometimes the hurtful things that are said aren't even true but they're said just to hurt you! And then there are the people who know when you're right about something but won't agree with you because they don't want to give you the satisfaction of being right. People will be in secret competitions with you all by themselves or just refuse to face their flaws.

Why would we put our needs in something so inconsistent like people? I'm guilty of doing the same thing when I was angry with others. That is why God has to be our everything. He is the same yesterday, today and forever. He is the truth and nothing anyone says has more value than what He says about you. We have to understand that human beings aren't perfect, and they aren't supposed to be. We still drop the ball sometimes even when we're trying not to be led by our emotions. Even by having just a quick thought. With that being said, it's nice to receive compliments, praises, and to be noticed, but it shouldn't be what fills you because only what God says about you is what truly matters.

This next point has been the hardest for me . . . not returning the offense but rising above it. I have realized that because God has given me the gift of prophecy, I see more than I would like to, and I speak the truth more than what's comfortable to others. I have caught a lot of shade for being straight up with people no matter how I deliver the message, with love or straight forwardness, I still get hit with the same exact response. Negativity. People have insulted my intelligence, my parenting, my education and my "status" with the Lord. I used to ALWAYS have a comeback and was pretty much ready for whatever that person wanted to do. God had to show me that if I clapped back when someone said or did something offensive, that meant I still needed some healing. [Side note: Did you know that how you treat people is a reflection of what's inside of you?] When I prayed to God, I was confused and frustrated because He was telling me what I could do better instead of what they could have done better. Even with the right heart posture the Lord would only speak about me and how He did not approve of the way I spoke to His people whether they "deserved" it or not. I have always had and still have a very big heart. I am for people. I'm a natural caretaker, so if my intentions were pure to begin with and I get slapped in the face with shade, why am I the one who needs to change? God showed me that because I returned what was given negatively to the person, I was defending myself. And for what? If I didn't believe what the person said was true then why retaliate, why explain myself, why run in circles or point fingers? What was I trying to prove to the person?

I'm a visual learner and I love that God takes the time to explain things to me so I can understand exactly what He's saying. God gave me a scenario one day. He showed me that my name was Breyonia Ashley Clark and then when I got married my name changed to Breyonia Ashley Brandon. If a stranger, or even a loved one, told me that my name was "Rachel Betty Moore," what would I do? So I thought, I would simply correct them. Then God asked me what if they got belligerent and called me a liar then what would I do? I thought about how I wouldn't even waste my time because how can anyone tell me what my name is or used to be? I'm me. God said, "Why is it any different in any other area of your life? You know who you are and who you're not." Was that deep or WHAT? God knows how to break it ALL the way down! This was a game changer for me. I will hold on to that word for the rest of my life.

Knowing who I am doesn't mean I don't get triggered. Every day, every moment of the day, I have to remember who God says I am. If you aren't exactly sure of who you are, like I wasn't for a while (and still learning), you have to find out. I had to press into God and dive deep into His Word to LEARN who I was. That's a whole different *book I have to write.* His Word literally tells us that we are loved, we are special, we are strong, we are fearless, we are courageous, we are heard, we are desired, we are protected, we are beautiful, we are more than a conqueror, we are free, we are forgiven, we are made new in Him, we are victorious through Christ, and we are children of the Most High. God loves EVERYTHING about us! He promises to make every sin or struggle clean. God promises to break us free and make us new. He does not turn His back or disown us. Anything that is counter to what God says is a lie. And just like how God can use people to bless and spread His truth, the enemy can use people as well to curse others and spread his lies. When you know who you are, no one can tell you otherwise. That's why Jesus handled the offenses with such grace. Like Jesus, we don't need to explain or defend ourselves. We can just let them talk and think what they want to. God KNOWS the truth and only His thoughts of you matter. Jesus knows who He is, do you?

Prayer:

Father God,

I thank You and praise You for Your grace and mercy. I thank You God for revealing Your truth to me. Father, I rebuke every lie the enemy has tried to have me believe that has caused doubt in where I stand with You. Father, I ask that You cleanse me from every lie that was planted from childhood up to this day. I ask that You cleanse me now, O God. Cleanse my heart and cleanse my mind with the blood of Jesus. I believe in Your word where You say that I am loved and accepted by You. So even if someone takes back what they said to hurt me, Lord, You said You will never leave me or forsake me. I believe that I am protected by You, so I have no fear because everything must bow to You. I believe that You are my provider, so I never have to worry about finances. You are my God, and You are known for making ways out of absolutely no way. I trust You, Lord, and today I make the decision to value Your thoughts of me over man.

In Jesus' mighty name, Amen.

Scriptures

Psalm 139:17, NIV
How precious also are your thoughts to me, O God! How great is the sum of them!

Matthew 10:29-31, NKJV
Are not two sparrows sold for a copper coin? And not one of them falls to the ground apart from your Father's will. But the very hairs of your head are all numbered. Do not fear therefore; you are of more value than many sparrows.

4

Called to Stay Home for a Season

"What do you do?" Family, friends or even strangers would ask me. Such a simple question, a fitting question in any normal conversation, but it felt like a gut punch every single time I was asked. I absolutely hated answering that question for two different reasons. The first reason was the TYPE of job I had, and the second reason would be me just not having a job.

As a child, I was pretty well-rounded. I wasn't perfect but I was clean, independent, and did well in school until I got pregnant at 16. Even when I was 16 and pregnant, I did pretty well to have graduated with my original class, and to be honest, I don't remember how I did it except that it had to be God. Can you imagine at age 17 getting up at five in the morning Monday through Friday to get ready for school? I had to get my son ready for daycare and be out before seven o'clock so my mom could beat the traffic. I would drop my son off, spend a full day at school, get picked up, watch my son while trying to study and get homework done, get him and myself ready for bed, and expect to be woken up out of my sleep every few hours to feed him until I had to get up and start the entire cycle again. Not to mention all the emotional stress I was under. All of it is a blur to me now except the reaction of one of my parents when I only graduated from high school with a C average.

On graduation day, there was a part in the ceremony when the principal wanted to recognize the students with the higher GPAs in our class by asking all the 4.0 and 3.0 GPA students to stand. I remember feeling the disappointment of one of my parents in the crowd because I didn't make the cut. Right after the ceremony one of my parents asked why I didn't have a special tassel or didn't make at least a B average. I felt a rush of shame and told them the truth. I simply responded that I got a D in Physiology, which was considered a college course.

My senior year was a very challenging year for me emotionally. It was extremely difficult for me to concentrate. I never struggled with that before. In hindsight, I shouldn't have been so hurt at my parent's reaction. Matter of fact, I should have seen that coming because when I brought home A's and B's, or 4's and 3's from elementary school, I was praised and treated special. Good grades to me meant attention and success. The attention and success I was getting for making good grades made me feel valued. It made me feel like I mattered. During most of my childhood I was admired for what I could do, and what I earned as a result of working hard. Don't get me wrong, my parents were and are loving, supportive and overall AMAZING parents. They were very old school and raised us similarly to how they were raised, which is expected, right? Traditions or in other words cycles . . . Honestly, I benefited a lot from the way I was raised because I learned that you work hard for what you want and persevere no matter what. If you know my siblings and I, you will see that we all have similar mindsets. Clarks don't ever give up and don't expect handouts.

The thing is, my parents expected more of me because they looked beyond my situation. I was a teenage mother and yet they still saw greatness in me. They believed in me more than I could believe in myself and they looked past where I was. I appreciate that more now than ever. Thank you, mommy and daddy! But what they didn't see is that I was stuck. I had dropped the ball, which is something I never did. Not only did I drop the ball, but I made a decision that was permanent. There was no turning back. I was hurt, angry, confused, depressed, lonely, ashamed, scared, frustrated, lost and desperate all at the same time. My parents pushed me to keep going out of the goodness of their hearts, but I pushed back because of the heartache I was experiencing. I pushed back because I didn't know who I was anymore. I didn't know until years later that I was actually depressed for years and as a result of the fact that I could no longer be the person to make A's and B's. I just wanted to fill myself up with so many things that don't even matter now: boys, sex, my social life, my appearance just to name a few. I even neglected my child's emotional needs during his early years. I was jacked up. A hot mess! All that to say, I made terrible choices and became stuck. Me being 28 as I write this book, and 29 in a few months, I still get a rush of anxiety and tempted with depression when I try to polish my resume. I am a stay-at-home mom unable to work a regular job because daycare is the amount I would make working, and quite honestly,

I'm sick of school. I feel traumatized by the fact that every time I start I can't seem to finish.

Even today, as a mother of three kids with no degree and no real work history, the simple four-worded question, "What do you do?" makes me feel that I am a nobody when my response is "I'm just a mom." I feel the same rush of shame I felt on my graduation day. I have nothing to SHOW, I have nothing to say. I love being a mother but nowadays that's simply not enough, as if being a mother isn't a full-time job all by itself. So, in this season, I keep to myself because I want to protect myself from having to face the shame of my husband supporting our family on his own. It's draining when you have to plan your conversation with someone beforehand to avoid certain questions. BUT GOD. One day He spoke to me so clearly. He said, "Change your perspective." I stared off in a glare trying to figure out what He meant and then I soon realized He heard my heart. I was on my laptop about to look for more jobs and silently started kicking myself for the mistakes of not getting my life in order when I had the opportunities to. How, after 11 years, am I in the same exact spot? Just a mom. When God said, "Change Your Perspective," again, I quickly grabbed a notebook because I knew He was about to download, and as expected this is what He said:

An Excellent Mother:
- Watches over her family
- Loves, nurtures, and corrects
- Prays and covers her family
- Feeds the family naturally and spiritually

- Cleans the home naturally and spiritually
- Creates order in the home
- Trains her children to be good people in the world (**multiply yourself**)
- Breaks generational strongholds
- LOVE in the purest form
- Watches her children grow up (children are the safest with their loving parents)

He also said, "Being a Mother is a ministry, a job I hired you for." Peace that I still can't describe to this day came over me. I was released from the enemy's grip keeping me bound by believing his lies. I was no longer bound by the belief that I wasted my life being a stay-at-home mother, that I shouldn't have had so many kids, and that I won't be able to have a life of purpose until my kids are older. I was finally free and felt proud that God called me to be a mother. Notice the list doesn't mention anything about perfection. It also didn't describe being an excellent mother. This list was custom made for MY situation and maybe even for just a season. Sometimes God calls certain parents to stay home and others not to. It's about the body of Christ so nobody has the same exact calling, and it doesn't make anyone less than or better than; it's just about being obedient to God, and listening to His voice and accepting His will for our lives over our own will.

In my heart I have always been a hard worker and never wanted to ask for help from anyone, not even my husband, but with my life being what it is in the natural I understand that God was teaching me to let go of pride and that He was pulling something bigger out of me spiritually.

God needed me home to fulfill the purpose He had for me. It's what birthed this book, my YouTube channel, and my Podcast. When it seems like you are stuck in a situation and you can't seem to get out of it yourself, seek God wholeheartedly. Let go of every negative emotion and seek God with an open heart and mind. Then He will begin to show you why.

Prayer:

Father God,

I thank You and praise You for the abundance of Your love. I thank You, Father, that You correct and use every mistake I have made and turn it around for my good. You are most powerful, Lord! There is literally nothing You can't do! Father, I thank You for seeing purpose in me even when the world doesn't. I accept Your truth over the lie of this world. Father, today I give You my will, my own desires of how my life is supposed to look and where I should be in this time of my life. I rid myself of my own timeline and open my heart to Yours. Father please show me why I am here in this season. I feel stuck but I believe there's a reason. Father clear my heart and my mind and speak to me Lord. Direct me on what to do in this time of stillness. I trust You, Father!

In Jesus' name, Amen.

Scriptures

Romans 8:28, NKJV

And we know that all things work together for good to those who love God, to those who are the called according to His purpose.

Jeremiah 29:11, NKJV

For I know the thoughts that I think toward you, says the Lord, thoughts of peace and not of evil, to give you a future and a hope.

5

Led by Emotions or Truth?

Don't bow to your emotions. We can be our OWN enemy preventing God's blessings because we are trusting our feelings over God. Feelings come and go, but God is consistent with His promises, His character, and His love. He's not like us and I'm glad He isn't to be honest, or we would all be in bad shape. We tend to trust others by the way they treat us. We are usually motivated to do something nice for those we have no issues with. God isn't like that. God is consistently loving and forgiving. When God asks us to do something and we hesitate, or like the old me and just flat-out rebel, because we didn't FEEL like it, we hinder our breakthroughs and blessings.

I was in a place where I didn't trust God, and not because I didn't want to, but because my emotions and my own understanding got the best of me. Trusting God is like walking on water as Peter did in Matthew 14:28-31. When Peter kept his focus on Jesus and put his trust in Him, Peter was able to step out of the boat and walk on water like Jesus. But once Peter took his sight off Jesus and focused on the wind blowing, he began to sink. God said trust Him but when I tried to take a step in faith, I quickly sank like Peter because it didn't make sense to me. I looked at my own wind, my situation, and didn't have faith. His ways are not our ways, His thoughts are not our thoughts. Like I said before, He's not human and that in itself is a blessing. I kept asking God how I could trust Him because I really wanted to. But I wondered how I could just trust Him when my feelings did not line up with what He was saying. It just wouldn't look or feel right. God simply said, "It's your emotions that you're bowing to." I was convicted and angry because I didn't know how to NOT bow to what I was feeling. Understanding God doesn't contradict Himself, if God says to trust Him and stop living in fear, Holy Spirit isn't going to tell you to run the opposite direction. That's not God.

I understood that I needed to be delivered from fear, but it wasn't just fear. I had to rid the partners of fear as well: anxiety, worry, stress, frustration, pride and control. It finally clicked that our emotions ARE NOT going to line up with our faith because our emotions are partners to our flesh! This means you may feel extremely uncomfortable. And honestly, it may even hurt being obedient to God. That's killing the flesh! I promise you when this finally clicked, my eyes were wide open. The enemy (even our flesh) is always going to oppose God because it's an enemy to God. The Word states that our carnal mind is hostile towards God (Romans 8:7), and my flesh would put up the biggest fight when wanting to do the right thing. I would get a rush of anxiety, anger, nausea, and even headaches when I said YES to God and NO to self.

Releasing all those spirits and fighting my flesh allowed God to be in full control. It allowed me to rest and to be in peace in the long run. It's not always the devil making it hard to fulfil God's will, sometimes it's us. Sometimes we stress ourselves out by unknowingly holding onto spirits that shouldn't be there. Unclean spirits will always egg us on to do the wrong thing, it's literally their job. Every thought and feeling doesn't have to be accepted, we have a choice!

In the Bible there are plenty of stories where people had to do extreme things that would have us freaking out and probably saying straight up NO! Think about it, Abraham was told to sacrifice his child (Genesis 22:2), Moses' mother had to send him down a river in a basket (Exodus 2:3), and David fought a giant with a slingshot and a stone (1 Samuel 17:49-51). There are way more stories, but the point is, these are acts of faith. Understand these people are human just like you and I, so that means they also had emotions and felt worse than what you probably felt just reading about what they had to do because it was their God-given instructions. I doubt they felt cheerful, excited, tickled or even understood why God would ask them to do these things, but they were still obedient. It's the same for us. Something that I learned, and I hope that it blesses you, is that no matter what God instructs us to do, we can rest assured that it will be okay for us in the end. We are human so it's natural to feel nervous and unsure, but that's the beauty of being a child of God, we don't have to be because of who our Heavenly Father is!

Prayer:

Father God,

I thank You and praise You for the revelation of my emotions. Right now, I surrender my flesh to You. Give me the desire to surrender to You instead of my emotions. I ask that You cleanse me from fear, control, pride, stubbornness, worry, anxiety and any other unclean spirits that tempt me to not obey Your word. I confess that I am stronger than my flesh in Jesus 'name! I don't want to stand in my own way anymore, O God. Fill me with Your spiritual fruits.

In Jesus' name, Amen.

Scriptures

Romans 12:2, NIV
Do not conform to the pattern of this world, but be transformed by the renewing of your mind. Then you will be able to test and approve what God's will is—his good, pleasing and perfect will.

2 Corinthians 5:7, NIV
For we walk by faith, not by sight.

6

Letting Go of Control

God gave me a dream where I was looking for my husband in this dark run-down looking place. In the dream, I knew my husband was someplace he shouldn't have been, but I wanted him with me. I wanted him with me so I could have peace of mind. In the dream, I went through this building and met this nice man who was so sweet. He was such a gentleman, and I could tell the man wanted me to slow down and talk to him. Instead of giving him my attention, I quickly pushed him to the side and said I need to find my husband first. I was relieved when I finally found my husband.

Sometimes we don't realize that WE may be the ones in the way of what God has for us. Whether it's mentally, emotionally, or physically, we can be chasing or holding onto something even when we don't know that we are. In her book *The Hannah Anointing: Becoming a Woman of Resilience, Fulfillment, and Fruitfulness,* Michelle McClain-Walters wrote, "Though we have demonic forces coming against us, some of the hindrances that cause the most damage come from within. They are like the little foxes that spoil the vine." Imagine God providing a ladder for you to climb to freedom, peace, and blessings. You're trying to climb with two large, heavy suitcases in each hand, an extremely heavy backpack, and a purse / man-bag that is way too heavy. You are now breathing hard, losing your footing, and having to keep restarting from the bottom. You're legitimately trying your best to go the way God has provided for you but it's extremely difficult. You begin to wonder why isn't God's way working? You are determined to reach what God has for you, so you are putting in 100% of the work and trusting Him, yet you still aren't getting anywhere. Why? Because you are literally being weighed down because your hands are full! The luggage you are carrying is filled with a bunch of heavy dead weight which is why you can't reach what God has waiting for you.

We need to let go of any and everything that is hindering us so that we can experience all that God has in store. God wants us to walk into what He has for us with no baggage, just free and clear with our trust rooted in Him. In the dream where I was looking for my husband, God was telling me that I needed to stop chasing my husband and stop worrying about what he is or isn't doing. The dream had more to it but what I want you to see is that even me focusing on my husband was added baggage. The gentleman in the dream was God and He wanted me to focus on Him and get to know Him in a more intimate way. I didn't understand the dream all the way at first because in my mind I was doing everything God expected of me, or so I thought. I would wake up talking to God; I fasted, listened to multiple sermons a day, had Bible study with the kids, read the Bible, prayed all throughout the day and tried my best to stay on top of my behavior. BUT in my heart, I was still worrying about my husband's walk with God and what I thought it should look like. I didn't want to give that part to God. I wanted to control as much as I could because I was afraid. I was afraid of my husband and me missing our blessings because he wasn't doing what I wanted. In my eyes my husband wasn't doing what I felt he needed to do. God then reminded me of the word about Mary and Martha.

In Luke 10:38-42, Martha invited Jesus to her home, and she went above and beyond to make sure Jesus was more than comfortable. I can only imagine how much labor she put in and I'm not even mad at her because I would have done the same exact thing. However, while she was doing all the work, her sister Mary was just sitting at Jesus' feet listening to His teachings. Martha was upset that she was doing all the work by herself and she let it be known. Jesus explained to Martha that what Mary was doing was actually something He appreciated. Not that Jesus didn't appreciate Martha's hospitality, He just didn't want Martha to be distracted by the little things, like He doesn't want us to be, too.

The most important thing as a believer is our intimacy with God and our obedience. The dream I had, exposed that I was distracted. I was being Martha distracted by what my husband was or wasn't doing and I needed to be Mary. I just didn't want to let it go though. The baggage I was carrying was control, fear, stress, worry, anger, and torment. I needed to see and know my husband was putting in the same amount of work that I was. I can't remember where I got this quote, but it said something like, "Letting go of control feels like putting on a blindfold and getting punched." That's EXACTLY how I felt. Staying on top of everything was ME protecting myself and making sure God was pleased with us as a couple so our family would be blessed instead of just trusting that He had us.

The first time God released me from my husband was early December 2019. Yes, I said the first time which means there were several times I had to release him because my walk was far from perfect. God told me to write out what I wanted in my husband. I didn't want to because I felt it was tedious. Even though it's true that God knows us better than we know ourselves, sometimes God will ask you to do things as an act of faith. He wants us to be obedient even when it doesn't make sense, so I did it. I began my list and to be honest I was a little annoyed when I started but once I was halfway into writing I started to feel differently. Something shifted in the most amazing way. My confidence was slightly higher, and I felt relieved, excited, and hopeful all at the same time. In other words, I immediately dropped the suitcases, backpack, and purse and started climbing the ladder God provided for me empty handed! I know my Heavenly Father's character so as I kept writing, I knew He was going to give me the desires of my heart! When I finished the list of my custom-made husband, I asked God to go on ahead and edit it. I was completely open to Him adding to the list or taking away from it as He saw fit. I put my complete trust in Him.

After writing the list, I went back and read it. I smiled knowing that I didn't have to stress anymore. Now that I decided to be intimate with the Lord and let go of the baggage, I was able to walk into freedom and blessings.

God's way taught me how to make Him my everything and allow Him to strengthen my weak areas. I had to let go of control so I could receive the blessings He has for me. Let go and let God!

Prayer:

Father,

I acknowledge that You are God. You are the Creator, and everything has to go through You before it happens. This world and everything in it, literally sits in the palm of Your hand. I know that to be true, but it can be hard to remember in times of stress. It's hard to remember when I see, feel, and hear the opposite of what You promised. Father help me to remember Your word and remember who You are to me. Help me remember that You will never allow anything to happen if it wasn't for my good. Help me to trust You, Your ways and Your instructions. Heal every part of me that makes it hard to trust You, Lord. Reveal to me where I need healing and forgiveness. God, I don't want to be in the way of what You have for me. I don't want to carry this burden of control anymore. The truth is I am afraid, O God. Please comfort me in Your Word and even supernaturally. Uproot everything that is coming against my faith in You.

In Jesus' mighty name, Amen.

Scriptures

Psalm 46:10-11, GW

Let go of your concerns! Then you will know that I am God. I rule the nations. I rule the earth. The LORD of Armies is with us. The God of Jacob is our stronghold.

1 Peter 5:7, NIV

Cast all your anxiety on him because he cares for you.

Philippians 4:6-7, NKJV

Be anxious for nothing, but in everything by prayer and supplication, with thanksgiving, let your requests be made known to God; and the peace of God, which surpasses all understanding, will guard your hearts and minds through Christ Jesus.

Proverbs 3:5, NKJV

Trust in the LORD with all your heart, And lean not on your own understanding.

7

Unrecognizable

When did I become this Bree? I honestly don't even recognize myself anymore. It's scary in a way because I can't even pinpoint when I got here. I know when I said yes to Christ, but I don't know when His word transformed me. It's kind of like puberty, I can't tell you when my breasts were formed, I just realized they were there one day. What I notice in myself today is the stuff that used to trigger me now tickles me. I don't necessarily laugh at a person or situation but at the spirit behind it. I'm still a work in progress but God has brought me so far from where I used to be in a very short amount of time. Like I said, I can pinpoint when I hit puberty spiritually (if that's even a thing), and can tell you how I got here.

In college I had this teacher that was super chill. Before a test she would give a study guide so we would know what to expect and that would narrow down the amount of studying we had to do. Then come test day, we were pleasantly surprised to see that the test was the EXACT study guide. She will always be appreciated for that! Not only was the studying for her tests not as broad

35

as other professors I had, but she also gave us the exact problems that she told us to study for, so we knew the exact answers. And Our God is the same way, believe it or not.

When we take our test called LIFE the Bible is our study guide filled with the correct answers to make sure we pass. The Bible will always be accurate to every situation we face because it's the Living Word. I wasn't sure what that meant at first, but it means the Bible is prophetic! It will always be relevant in any and everything you face in life. We may not have the exact time frame as far as dates and times of the day, but stories in the Bible are similar to the story of our lives.

Through the Bible, God is literally telling us what His plans are for us and why we face certain situations in our lives. God revealed His plan to place Joseph in a position of authority, but before that would come into play Joseph was sold into slavery by his brothers, lied on, and imprisoned. Another example is Paul who was once known as Saul when he persecuted Christians. Paul had an encounter with Jesus that converted him, and he began to preach the gospel. The Bible will also give you great advice and understanding on how to move through life and make the right decision. Although she could have died by the hands of her husband, king Ahasuerus, I know that's hard to pronounce, Esther listened to her cousin Mordecai and spoke up on behalf of the Jews to save their lives. The Word of God is living and still gives us advice on who we are and what it is we should do.

Take it from me, the Word of God speaks to you better than your closest friend, mentor, spouse or parent. When I got tired of failing the same test over and over, I turned to the Bible as my very last resort and found the answers to life. It's sad but true. I looked to others for direction and that's what kept me walking in circles. At that time in my life the people that I was confiding in weren't all the way healed themselves. They were only able to give me what they had, half-truths and brokenness. Why? Because you attract who you are. When I was at the end of myself, I began to read the Word for answers. I needed answers and guidance. Then I wanted to pray and I fast. The appetite came when I finally tasted the Lord for myself and saw He was actually good. *The Word says, " Oh, taste and see that the LORD is good; Blessed is the man who trusts in Him!"* (Psalm 34:8, NKJV).

I did more to feed my spirit instead of doing other things that would feed my flesh like complain, eat, and indulge in entertainment. I can confidently say that I have grown so much over the years that I don't recognize myself anymore. I thank God for every obstacle because I would not be who I am without all that I have faced. I would not be so quick to pray and trust God in every situation of my life. Sometimes we believe the lie of the enemy when we are in difficult situations but it's honestly the best place to be. For some of us it takes discomfort to remember who God is and that is the point. Rude awakenings are meant for growth in Christ.

Prayer:

Father,

Thank You so much for Your living Word that I have full access to whenever! Thank You, Lord, for loving me so much when I was steadily undeserving of Your love and kindness. God thank You for being a God of second chances and calling me even in my mess. Thank You for seeing the past where I am but seeing me for who I will be! God continue to mold me into the person You have called me to be. Renew my mind each and every day, purify my heart so that You are pleased with me, O God. My deepest desire is to serve You with my life, O God. This second time around You showed me what really matters in this life and it's none of what I placed over You. Lord keep me under Your hand. Lord don't let me be without You ever in Jesus' name. I magnify Your name in my life and I humble myself to You Lord.

In Jesus' name, Amen and Amen.

Scriptures

2 Corinthians 5:17, NKJV

Therefore, if anyone is in Christ, he is a new creation; old things have passed away; behold, all things have become new.

Colossians 3:9-11, NKJV

Do not lie to one another, since you have put off the old man with his deeds, and have put on the new man who is renewed in knowledge according to the image of Him who created him, where there is neither Greek nor Jew, circumcised nor uncircumcised, barbarian, Scythian, slave nor free, but Christ is all and in all.

Lamentations 3:22-24, NKJV
Through the Lord's mercies we are not consumed. Because His compassions fail not. They are new every morning; Great is Your faithfulness. "The Lord is my portion," says my soul, "Therefore I hope in Him!"

8

Is God Enough?

"Will you be willing to lose your identity for me?" This is what God asked me the day after I began ministering outside of my home. At first, I wasn't sure what He meant by that question. Then I felt a sense of anxiety at the thought of what my community would think of me after they saw what I've been working on this entire time. For some reason I didn't see them being proud because I was no longer the Breyonia they knew for 28 years. She died. Who I am now is someone who looks to God for everything, someone who has crazy faith in Jesus, someone who isn't afraid of dying, someone who wants to help instead of condemning, someone who wants to pray instead of gossip, someone who wants to honor God in everything I do. I became what would be considered "over the top" for Christ especially for my age.

Before the death I thought I was free, healed and done caring about what others thought of me. When I say God knows us better than we know ourselves that is the 100% honest truth. When God presented this question, it revealed that I wasn't as healed as I thought. The fact that I felt anxiety because of what my family and friends may say or thought of me was unnerving. My being concerned about their thoughts of me over God's thoughts was clear that I still had some more healing to let God do. If I were to be completely honest, I am scared of myself! I'm still not familiar or even comfortable with who I am. Just to be clear, I LOVE who I have become but it's still different. It's still something I'm getting used to, you know?

The passage where the man tells Jesus that he needed to bury his father and Jesus' reply, "let the dead bury the dead" (Luke 9:60), was never as clear as it was to me until now. As harsh as that text seems, it's really Jesus exposing what is in our hearts. It's what He exposed about me regarding my family! All my life I have always loved being with family. I always wanted everyone to be good. I always wanted to plan everything and make it special by sacrificing what I needed. I didn't think it was wrong because that's what family is for, but it was actually unhealthy the way I was going about it. It was all rooted in fear of not being accepted.

The fear of not belonging and being alone was why I would go above and beyond for people. In some twisted way, feeling needed made me feel wanted, liked, and desired. There is a difference though. God exposed to me that I had others before Him. He showed me that I wanted others more than I wanted Him. I needed to let my family go and draw closer to Him. God needed to be my EVERYTHING. Making the adjustment for God to be my everything was a hard adjustment. It requires having a mindset like Christ. It's not easy at first but it's possible, and as we continue to unlearn every lie it gets easier. For me unlearning lies looked like letting go of expectations of man because they will always fail me. I had to make up in my mind that God was my everything. Unlike human beings, our God is so patient and gentle that He doesn't discard us when we make Him angry. He doesn't just watch us suffer for His own entertainment or gossip about us. God always keeps His promises, and when He gives it's out of His goodness with no strings attached. God even blesses those that curse Him. His sun even rises on those who are evil and good, and it rains on them both (Matthew 5:45). I'm so grateful for that.

When God asked me to give up my identity for Him, my answer was YES! I am now a Kingdom woman. I'm not Breyannia Clark, Yannia Bree, or even Breyonia Brandon. Those names mean nothing more than what is necessary on Earth. Yes, my mother and father had me and raised me, and I grew up with my siblings and all that good stuff. We have a lot of beautiful moments and memories, and I truly love them, but they can't come before my God. Family was my idol. The way that I valued them was hindering me from being all that God called me to be.

It's the same for my husband and my kids, they cannot, and will not, ever come before God. It's like that Abraham and Isaac moment. God is asking me to sacrifice all that I've ever known regarding family, friends, and community. The love is there but idolatry isn't. I don't believe God is asking that I cut my family off and be done with them forever. He's asking me to let go of the comfort and the validation I thought I needed from them. He will provide everything I need like the ram in the bush. I trust Him and His validation is more than enough. Is God enough for you?

Prayer:

Father God,

Thank You, thank You, thank You for Your love and kindness. You are truly too good for words, O God. I ask that You forgive me for thinking that what others think or feel about me matters more than You. Forgive me for wanting to be accepted by the creations more than the Creator of all! God, I repent right now, O God, for placing You in every other place but first in my life. Father, I realize just how great You really are. You are so worthy God and I owe You everything I have, everything I am and everything that's within me! God, I dedicate my life to You. Help me to walk according to Your will. Guide me Lord. I want to be pleasing in Your sight Jesus. I thank You and praise You.

In Jesus's name, Amen and Amen.

Scriptures

Matthew 8:22, NIV
But Jesus told him, "Follow me, and let the dead bury their own dead.

Luke 9:23, NIV
Then he said to them all: "Whoever wants to be my disciple must deny themselves and take up their cross daily and follow me.

9

Let's Purge

The physical act of something can actually impact what happens in the spirit, an example would be getting baptized. The physical act of being submerged under water represents death (dying to the flesh), and coming up out of the water is being born again in the Spirit. The entire process represents the person is no longer of the flesh but is now living by the Holy Spirit. I hope that makes sense. In the same way, there was a period in my life where I felt terrible due to the amount of warfare I was facing.

One day God instructed me to clean my room and bathroom. I'm far from messy, I'm actually a neat freak, but God called me to do something like spring cleaning. I began to throw away old things that were not being used. Turns out, I had a lot of things I did not use anymore. In that moment I began to feel better instantly! It was like what I mentioned earlier, the act of doing something physically can impact things spiritually. Throwing away old, unnecessary things in the natural made me feel like I was throwing away things I was holding onto emotionally, mentally, and even spiritually. As I write this now, God is telling me I was making room for new and better things He has for me! After getting rid of old clothes, hair products and other stuff, I started to rearrange things. Having a clean environment represented a new and improved Bree.

Cleaning and decluttering just made me feel better all around. I even wanted to clean and change my entire apartment, but time flew by and I had to stop and tend to my children. Tempted to get frustrated, God reminded me that it's a process. He told me to be proud of what I did accomplish in my bedroom and bathroom and it's the same with healing mentally, emotionally and spiritually. It is a process.

As much as we wish we can be healed and pain-free in a day, we have to be patient with ourselves and God. We must focus and be proud of what we DID accomplish mentally, emotionally, or physically. We know all God has to do is speak it and whatever He desires will come to pass, so why doesn't He do that with us when we are all jacked up? Why does it feel like He just wants us to suffer instead of rescuing us? I've learned that God will take His time with us so that we will be complete! Completely healed, completely free, completely faithful to Him . . . just complete. It's because there needs to be some character behind being free. In my wilderness season my character changed tremendously. I didn't know that I was actually a brat, selfish, controlling, deeply angry, holding on to unforgiveness and codependent. I truly didn't know until I suffered; until I felt pain and I was uncomfortable.

To me, purging meant that I would have a neater closet, new bathroom setting, rearranged bedroom, but the process was actually a symbol of me forgiving myself, rejecting lies I've held on for years and accepting people for who they were. It also meant that I now had freed up some space for God to bless me, remember?! I was now able to lean on God and grow. All that in one day of cleaning and that was just the beginning.

So much more of what God has for us is waiting on the other side of everything we face. We just have to stay in God's face and keep holding His hand. Every trial, rejection, and hurt is a steppingstone to the blessings that God has for us. I'm now desperate for peace, joy, stability, safety and a healthy amount of self-worth, wouldn't you agree? Let's Purge!

Prayer:

Father God,

You are the ultimate healer! I thank You and praise You for who You are and that nothing is too hard for You. I ask You Father to purge us inside out. Right now, I open myself to You, Jesus Christ, to remove everything that's not of You. God remove from me the terrible things that have happened to me, hurtful things that were said to me, generational traumas, things that I have learned to be, and even things I decided to be from hurt. I ask that You remove it all, O God. I ask You, Lord, to create in me a clean heart. I ask that You burn away everything that doesn't bring You glory. Refill me with You, O God. I thank You for the complete work You are doing in me. I thank You for being the God of second chances and I give You all the honor and glory.

In Jesus name, Amen and Amen.

Scriptures

Romans 12:2, NIV
Do not conform to the pattern of this world, but be transformed by the renewing of your mind. Then you will be able to test and approve what God's will is--his good, pleasing and perfect will.

Ephesians 4:22-24, NKJV
... that you put off, concerning your former conduct, the old man which grows corrupt according to the deceitful lusts, 23 and be renewed in the spirit of your mind, 24 and that you put on the new man which was created according to God, in true righteousness and holiness

Galatians 3:27, NIV
For all of you who were baptized into Christ have clothed yourselves with Christ.

Matthew 9:17, NASB
Nor do people put new wine into old wineskins; otherwise the wineskins burst, and the wine pours out and the wineskins are ruined; but they put new wine into fresh wineskins, and both are preserved.

10

Broken People Break People

It's really not entirely them. You know the people who mistreat you. People will allow the enemy to use them and not even realize it. I am definitely not supporting people's wrongdoings; I just want this to help you let go of any hurt that you can't seem to let go of.

One day, as an adult, I was trying to figure out why whenever I was looked over, while with another person or people, I felt less than or insecure? God showed me that being looked over triggered the wounds from childhood that had never been addressed. I'm sure I wasn't the only one, but I was that girl who would like boys that didn't like her back. I had inconsistent friends who would be my best friend one day and my enemy the next. I know even for me looking back at this I'm like, "no big deal," but clearly it still had some effect on me as an adult.

The thing is, even though it's not a big deal to me now, it was a huge deal growing up. My heart was always different from other kids and I realize that now. As I grew up, I learned to mask my wounds with "false confidence." Just like any wound we get physically we need to clean it first so it will heal properly. Putting numbing cream or just a bandage on a wound will not promote the wound to heal properly. It temporarily relieves pain and masks it, but the wound still isn't clean. We know that an unclean wound will later cause infections or some other complications. In a 2019 article by Jayne Leonard for Medical News Today, she states, "If a person does not receive treatment for a wound infection, it can spread to other parts of the body. Which may lead to serious complications." I believe it's the same emotionally and spiritually and I was "infected" for years.

Getting braces, waist trainers, looking up mommy makeover surgeries and wearing revealing clothes was supposed to make me feel better. Don't get me wrong, I don't believe anything is wrong with it if you're doing any of this for yourself and only yourself. If that's what you like then that's what you like, BUT for me, after searching my heart, the truth was, I wanted to be noticed and desired by others. I used my body to prove I was beautiful and worth looking at. Let me tie all of this together . . .

Since kindergarten, I have been called ugly or made fun of for something I had no control over. I teased others as well, but for years of being told I wasn't pretty or good enough I believed it. I didn't like my dark shadowy eyes, my long and skinny legs, my petite figure, or my thick coarse hair. And don't get me started on my crooked teeth. Being made fun of even by adults was doing more damage than I was conscious of. It's why I wanted to wear revealing clothes or even expose my naked body to men who didn't have to work hard to see it. I wanted to be noticed, liked, desired, and accepted. That's why it triggered me when people overlooked me. I asked God how I could stop feeling this way? God said so clearly, "Stop believing the enemy's lie." I responded, "God, I know, but how? I know you said I was made in your image and that You think I'm beautiful, but I want to see it, too." I then had a flash of an article I read that spoke about how the enemy can attack us with our own eyes. The enemy can literally prevent us from seeing what's true like our beauty for example. Have you ever met someone who was really attractive and they literally didn't see it? Not the person who acts like they don't see they are attractive so that you can compliment them more, but someone who is really blinded from the truth. It is because the enemy has taken their vision of seeing what God has made them to be. God then tied that flash back with telling me that the enemy had literally used every single person who said I wasn't good enough. Every person who said that I was too tall, too thin, too dark or only good for what I can do with my body. They were ALL lies. Every single one!

I find it no surprise now because I understand broken people will try and break people. You know the saying, "misery loves company?" It's the same thing. Those people who ALLOWED the enemy to use them were hurt because they also believed the lies. Like I said, I even talked about people because I wasn't happy with myself. It's a vicious cycle that needs to be addressed. The truth is that God made us in His image. God decided what we would look like, and since we are His children, He looks at us and sees perfection.

If you're a parent, it's similar to how you look at your own children. You truly believe your son is handsome or daughter is beautiful because they're yours. Then I thought, what if the way God looks at us is deeper than what we see in the physical? What if God looks at our soul and only sees the soul? Something that can't be seen with just our eyes. How we are able to see a person's soul is through their conversation, their attitude, the way they carry themselves, and their fruit! That is the exact thing we don't usually look at in others or even ourselves. Why? Because, yet again, the enemy tells us women, for example, that we are considered beautiful if we have straight teeth, nice perky breasts, a flat tummy with a slim waist, and a round butt. It's not that we shouldn't want to be in shape due to health reasons, but if we believe that our identity is solely on how we look on the outside, we are believing lies from the enemy and not God's truth. When we find ourselves seeking validation from others or comparing ourselves to others, we need to really look into ourselves and ask why? Society has brainwashed us into believing the enemy's lies so don't be hard on yourself. If it turns out that you are dealing with the same issue, you need to go and have a one-on-one talk with God. He will show you the truth.

It has been a task for me to remind myself and relearn what I believe about myself. But it has become easier as I continue to flush out the years of lies I believed by meditating on what God says about me in His Word. I encourage you to do the same because broken people only know how to tell you the same lies they believe about themselves.

> For You formed my inward parts;
> You covered me in my mother's womb.
> I will praise You, for I am fearfully *and* wonderfully made;
> Marvelous are Your works,
> And *that* my soul knows very well.
> Psalm 139:13-14, NKJV

Prayer:

Father, in the name of Jesus,

I thank You for creating me in Your image. Hallelujah, I praise You for being so good to me! Father, I repent for believing the enemy's lie and trying to be everything You have not created me to be. I repent for considering others' thoughts of me above Your thoughts of me. I ask that You forgive me for these things in Jesus' mighty name. Father, I forgive those who have been used by the enemy for saying hurtful things to me from the earliest offense to even now, O God. I release the pain of every hurtful word and I accept Your truth of what You say and think of me. I am free from the lies of the enemy! Help me to see myself the way You see me. Teach me to love myself so that I can love others, O God. I break the vicious cycle of emotional abuse, psychological abuse, and spiritual abuse. I am only who You say I am, Lord!

In Jesus' name I pray, Amen and Amen!

**Something that has helped me to relearn the truth of what God says is seeing it every day. So, I write on every mirror what God says. Below are some scriptures that you can write on your mirror with a DRY ERASE MARKER. It's fun and healing. Just a reminder every time you see yourself.

Scriptures

Ephesians 1:5, NIV
He predestined us for adoption to sonship through Jesus Christ, in accordance with his pleasure and will-

Psalm 46:5, NIV
God is within her, she will not fall; God will help her at break of day.

1 Peter 3:3-4, NIV
Your beauty should not come from outward adornment, such as elaborate hairstyles and the wearing of gold jewelry or fine clothes. Rather, it should be that of your inner self, the unfading beauty of a gentle and quiet spirit, which is of great worth in God's sight.

Proverbs 3:15-18, NIV
She is more precious than rubies; nothing you desire can compare with her. Long life is in her right hand; in her left hand are riches and honor. Her ways are pleasant ways, and all her paths are peace. She is a tree of life to those who take hold of her; those who hold her fast will be blessed.

Songs 4:7, NIV
You are altogether beautiful, my darling; there is no flaw in you.

2 Timothy 1:7, NIV
For the Spirit God gave us does not make us timid, but gives us power, love and self-discipline.

2 Corinthians 3:18, NIV
And we all, who with unveiled faces contemplate the Lord's glory, are being transformed into his image with ever-increasing glory, which comes from the Lord, who is the Spirit.

Romans 12:2, NKJV
Do not be conformed to this world, but be transformed by the renewal of your mind, that by testing you may discern what is the will of God, what is good and acceptable and perfect.

Ephesians 1:4-6, NIV
For he chose us in him before the creation of the world to be holy and blameless in his sight. In love he predestined us for adoption to sonship through Jesus Christ, in accordance with his pleasure and will—to the praise of his glorious grace, which he has freely given us in the One he loves.

1 Peter 2:9, NIV
But you are a chosen people, a royal priesthood, a holy nation, God's special possession, that you may declare

the praises of him who called you out of darkness into his wonderful light.

John 15:15-16, NIV

I no longer call you servants, because a servant does not know his master's business. Instead, I have called you friends, for everything that I learned from my Father I have made known to you. You did not choose me, but I chose you and appointed you so that you might go and bear fruit—fruit that will last—and so that whatever you ask in my name the Father will give you.

1 Corinthians 6:20, NKJV

You were bought at a price. Therefore honor God with your bodies.

Isaiah 43:1, NKJV

But now thus says the Lord, he who created you, O Jacob, he who formed you, O Israel: Fear not, for I have redeemed you; I have called you by name, you are mine.

11

The Art of Life

I truly thank God for every trial, every attack, every betrayal, every closed door and every tear I have cried in THIS season!! All of it has produced so much of God's fruit and strengthened me in ways I could have never imagined. Difficult situations have made me wiser. This season has opened my eyes to truth, and has shown me my purpose and brought me to where I should have always been. When God allows us to go through the fire, it doesn't make sense to us, but He knows what He's doing. He knows what's necessary so that we will be blessed, and He is glorified. It's always a win-win for those who stay with the Lord.

Have you ever watched an artist named Bob Ross paint a picture? When he starts painting you have no idea where he's going with the random streaks on the blank canvas. But that's the thing, it's not random to Bob because he sees something we don't. He knows how to get his painting to look exactly the way he wants it to. Most importantly, he knows what he's doing even when it makes no sense to us. He knows what types of brushes to use, what types of colors to mix, where to fade colors, how much pressure to apply, etc.

It's the same with God. God paints our lives as beautiful masterpieces that we criticize when we face challenges in life simply because we cannot see the finished picture. We don't understand the process of God's creation of our lives. We don't understand why God would have us apply for jobs just to be rejected, why God would instruct us to speak to people who will only mock us, or even why God would allow a pregnancy only to miscarry. It's His way of switching brushes, mixing colors, fading colors, or a sudden switch in streaks. We have to trust that we are in the best hands, and that He is creating beautiful masterpieces that will have us simply amazed when we begin to understand, or should I say see, what He's doing. If only we could just sit and watch Him work in peace. Easier said than done, right?

One of my favorite characters in the Bible is Joseph. Joseph knew he had a calling on his life at such an early age and because of that he stood out. He was even treated differently than his brothers which didn't make it easier for him. What God allowed him to go through was extremely rough BUT at the end he was made Ruler. Talk about from pit to palace or rags to riches! I encourage you to read the story, I believe it will encourage you like it did me. But like Joseph, we have to wait on God and trust the process. Sometimes when we get impatient, we throw our hands up and say, "fine, God, I will do it myself."

I imagine it looking like us coming in painting some broccoli looking trees and yellow corner suns to speed up the process. It's the best we can do because we are doing things in our own strength and with our own understanding. With God being God, He gets the last say. So, I imagine with His gentleness, He lets us paint and have our way for a moment and then goes back to paint over/correct the mess we made. He takes our ordinary and makes it extraordinary. In hardship we settle for the bare minimum when God has more than what could be thought of because of our impatience. Like children we want instant gratification. I can only speak on this because I have been here myself way too many times. And praise God for sending people in my life to talk me off of some ledges. But aren't we blessed to serve a loving Father who will STILL come through and give us better when we try to settle for less? During the process, while He's painting out our lives, God wants us to focus on loving Him, knowing Him, and allowing Him to work in His own way and time. In other words, God wants us to completely trust His skills, His abilities, and His faithfulness even when we don't understand, agree, or SEE what He's doing. God will not Fail Us!

Prayer:

Father, in the name of Jesus,

I thank You and praise You simply for who You are. Thank You, God, for choosing me. Father, I repent for every time that I have gone ahead of You to do things my way because I was impatient and uncomfortable. Father, I also repent for complaining and not trusting You. I ask that You help me to trust You and wait on You, Lord. I know that I can't see what

You're doing and how things are going to end, but naturally where I am it's overwhelming and I need relief. Supernaturally give me all that I am lacking so that I can stand, so that I can believe. Lord, I give You my concerns, my feelings and even my frustrations as I wait on You. I know that You love me and won't ever allow me to go through anything if it wasn't for my benefit. So, I will rest on You and trust that You will never leave my side. Thank You for Your patience and STILL giving me more than I could ever think or ask.

In Jesus' name, Amen.

Scriptures

Jeremiah 28:11, NLT
For I know the plans I have for you," says the Lord. "They are plans for good and not for disaster, to give you a future and a hope.

12

Disguised Compliment

You wear this nice outfit and your friend can only find something negative to say or says, "That outfit would look better on me." You share your weight-loss journey to encourage an associate, but instead of listening they suddenly have to go. You start a project and share it with your friend expecting them to support you, however, they never mention it. They only want to talk about what's going on with them. You feel tension with a person when you share your happiness. You get the point, right? All of these examples could leave you feeling some type of way, especially when it's a consistent pattern. It's no big deal at first, but when there's a constant dose of shade it gets to be a bit much.

BUT guess what? If we decide to stop sitting in what the rejection looks and feels like we can understand that it could actually be taken as a compliment. Obviously, this may not be true in everything like dating or an interest in a job or school. There may be some legitimate reasons as to why you are being rejected or denied. The rejection I'm talking about is the one you experience in relationships with family, friends, and associates. People you believe love and care about you. I have experienced this type of rejection as early as childhood and now as an adult it would trigger me badly. In response, I would end up saying or doing something passive aggressive. A complete waste of time in hindsight and kind of embarrassing now that I think about it. The truth was that being rejected hurt my feelings.

After sitting at God's feet, a bunch of different times crying, whining, screaming and groaning, God showed me that being rejected did not mean I was not valued. What if we changed our mind and chose not to internalize the direct or indirect shade? You can look at it as that person rejecting your joy because they are miserable; that they are rejecting your accomplishments because they don't have what you're gaining, or that the person is simply rejecting you because your presence causes them to feel less than. The point is that when you expect certain people to be there for you, and instead they reject you, it may be because they are hurt and or jealous. Either way it is them not you. Sometimes if someone has been playing the devil's advocate for so long, they don't know how to simply be happy for someone else.

To this day, I experience rejection and I'm learning to get used to it. I had to learn to be comfortable with who God has created me to be, so that I do not need anyone else's validation. And honestly, I don't know if it's a prophet thing, but I had to be content with God being my everything because being rejected comes with the calling. I had to accept that I was to be the one to support and push people into greatness and not get that in return. One of the hardest truths I had to accept was that EVERYONE IS NOT LIKE ME. It is the same for you, if you are the type of person who has a big heart! Jesus wasn't accepted into His own town either (John 4:44, Luke 4:16-30, Matt. 13:54-57). And I just want to point something out; notice how much "love" you get when you're broken, struggling, and living in the world versus saying yes to Christ and allowing Him to transform you. There's something to be said about people only liking you when you're not doing better than them.

You are set apart though. When you know you love hard, you truly want the best for others and are legitimately happy for them. It really sucks that people refuse or simply cannot give it back to you in return, but the good news is that you will always have Jesus and His Kingdom rooting for you. Remember this is a disguised compliment! It means that you ARE doing a great job. Continue to let the Lord use you!

Prayer:

Father, in the name of Jesus,

Help me to forgive the people I have expected to be supportive and loving. Help me to forgive those who were only in my life to be entertained by my struggles or to feel better about themselves. Lord it hurts to be the one to support people and not get that in return. Father, I ask that You be my everything from this day forward, and support me in my growth in You and in other places in my life. I ask that You send like-minded people as well

Lord, in Jesus' name. People who will have a true heart and not be jealous of what You are doing in my life.

In Jesus name, Amen and Amen.

Scriptures

1 Peter 2:9, NIV
But you are a chosen people, a royal priesthood, a holy nation, God's special possession, that you may declare the praises of him who called you out of darkness into his wonderful light.

13

Heard the Lie, Felt the Truth

Have you ever felt like a target? In the season that I'm writing this, my "broken heart" is constantly aching from blow after blow of disappointments. I begin to question God, and I know I shouldn't but it's more of what am I supposed to get out of this? You know the famous "why me Lord" cry? I begin to wonder if I'm missing something. I begin to think I am the problem and that something is wrong with me because I am the common denominator in every situation.

Everyone seemed to be having issues with me because of my mouth. The crazy thing is, I try not to say much because of this very issue, animosity with others. I promise you that I rehearse conversations a million times in my head. I dissect every piece of what was said, wondering if I misunderstood something, if I assumed incorrectly, or if I said the wrong thing or said the right thing wrong.

Seldom do I blame someone else when there's a conflict. I am super hard on myself because I don't like conflict, beef, or whatever you call it. PLEASE don't get me wrong! I am not peachy perfect! I have hurt people, used people, lied to people so this isn't a moment where I cry

65

victim. I am not perfect, nobody is. What prompted me to write this chapter was because I was being hurt by people who constantly lied to me for no reason. I'm talking about the kind of lies people tell that will have you questioning your sanity or in my case your discernment.

God spoke to me. He told me I'm not the problem even though I was the common denominator. God told me that I am a solution. I became a target for the kingdom of darkness because I am a threat to the enemy. I was a threat because I was able to discern the truth. God showed me how the enemy used my abandonment issues to prevent me from believing what God would show me through discernment. I needed to be accepted by others and that is the saddest place to be. I didn't want to disagree with people or step on their toes, so I would just go along with whatever. It was something I felt since I was a little girl when things were off. As I got older, I would ignore my gut feelings because I was afraid to be alone. And then what does our God do? Isolate me. He isolated me in every way possible just to expose the lie of the enemy.

I would have never changed into the woman of God I am today if God didn't allow me to be afflicted so greatly in 2018-2020. The crazy thing was that these weren't the only hurtful years of my life, but they are the most memorable because I said YES to God. They were the most memorable because I handled my pain differently. I chose to grow in pain, and because of that I became a new person. My entire life has been filled with me swapping "best friends" to be my source of love in whatever season I was in. I was so desperate for attention and acceptance that I didn't care what it cost to get it. Even if it cost my peace and my joy. Even if it was never real.

When I was everyone's enemy at what felt like the same time, I ran to God for answers only because I got tired of trying to figure it out myself. I knew that this had to be bigger than me because how can someone who aims to only please people be rejected from everyone? This is what happens when you sacrifice your life for people, in return you get emptiness. You become bound to this never-ending cycle of pleasing others so that you can *feel* like you belong, but IT NEVER LASTS. People will love you and like you for what you can do for them instead of who you are. It's not even their fault because we are the ones who allow it. It sucks but the truth is we didn't really know any better.

As a kid, I would do my best to express how I felt, but I was either shut down, criticized, laughed at or lied to. People will tell you anything and make you believe you are crazy or too sensitive just so you won't see what's really in their heart. Some people just refuse to be accountable for their actions. I get it because it's why I didn't believe what I discerned in people and chose to believe whatever I was told. I always had the gift to hear someone say one thing but felt what was in their heart. I would just lie to myself because I didn't want to believe someone would be so cruel to me. In either case, a lie is a lie. It's the same issue of refusing truth. There is something wrong with **only** seeing the good in people. The enemy knew I had abandonment issues and so speaking what I felt, or what God showed me, would risk being abandoned. I would never risk that because I needed to be accepted.

From 2018 to 2020, God needed me to be in a place where I was rejected. I needed the people closest to me to hurt me because I needed to be gracefully broken. The pain put me in a place where I didn't care what people said about me, what they thought of me, or even felt about me anymore. I learned to TRUST what God was showing me instead of what someone said to me. He needed me in a position to see and understand so that I can intercede, especially for those who could not see their own truth. Trusting the Holy Spirit has given me so much peace. I'm free from bondage, control, and even fear. God has shown me that He trusts me with more because He has shown me more about others. He showed me more not to gossip, judge, or condemn, but to give me an understanding of how to intercede in prayer for that person, how to interact with that person, what to expect from that person, and even how to set proper boundaries. I am no victim because I allowed what happened to me. Even though I didn't know any better, I am so glad that I do now. I'm so in love with the person God has shaped me to be. Like Marvin Sapp said, "I'm stronger, I'm wiser, I'm better, so much better."

Prayer:

Father, in the name of Jesus,

Thank You for being the light that exposes truth! Thank You for never leaving Your children in a dark place of confusion, hurt, or even desperation. Father, I pray right now that You take away every ounce of pain from childhood to this very day that has caused me to be so desperate that I ignore the truth. Father open my eyes, my mind, and my heart to be able to receive all that I need to know without rejecting it, so that I will be transformed into what You have called me to be. I thank You, Father, that everything that happens to me, good or bad, that You are there and that You work it out for my good. I'm so thankful that even in hard times Father You are there and that I can hold on to Your promises with confidence that You will do exactly what You said because You are not a man that lie! I'm so grateful to be in Your hands. Thank You, Jesus.

In Jesus mighty name, Amen and Amen!

Scriptures

2 Timothy 2:7, NASB
Consider what I say, for the Lord will give you understanding in everything.

Psalm 119:66, NKJV
Teach me good discernment and knowledge, For I believe in Your commandments.

1 Kings 3:9, NKJV
So give Your servant an understanding heart to judge Your people to discern between good and evil. For who is able to judge this great people of Yours?"

1 Kings 4:29, NASB
Now God gave Solomon wisdom and very great discernment and breadth of mind, like the sand that is on the seashore.

14

It Goes Both Ways, Humble Yourself

Pride is a sneaky spirit that slips in almost anywhere if you are not cautious. In the season that I'm writing this, I feel like things have been moving and God has been transforming me into the woman He's been calling me to be. Today, He gently reminded me that I still have ways to go. I was caught off guard when He gave me this word because personally, I don't even recognize myself anymore. That is how much I have let my old ways go. What was God referring to when He said I still have ways to go? Was God not pleased with me? I began to wonder what I did wrong because I have been intentional up to this point about everything and quickly repenting when I did wrong. God then revealed to me that it was not the obvious. There was still pride in my heart. No, I didn't think I was better than my husband or anyone for that matter. God showed me how I look at my husband, expecting and waiting for change so we can move in our marriage. God shows me I'm still in a place that needs improvement as well. When He first told me that I became angry, but then it convicted me deeply.

We usually compare ourselves to who we once were. Because we made changes, and based on what we see and others haven't, we can believe that we are better or higher than them. Truth is, if we compare the new us to Jesus, we suddenly don't look like we did too much. It is truly humbling. This is not to discourage you but to simply remind you that we can't judge the next person. We cannot compare ourselves to anyone but Jesus. We all need to focus on our own walks and support each other to grow and be better than we were yesterday.

It is challenging when we make changes and still get treated the same, but it's because we are holding ourselves in a place of God. Our response is kind of like, "How could you do that, when I have done this?" when really the one who is able to have that type of stance is God, and the crazy thing is He doesn't even do that to us. He corrects us, He forgives us, and He loves us. Our flesh tells us that we *deserve* to be treated a certain way, but doesn't that sound similar to Satan? Satan believed he deserved praise that belonged to God. He expected the same treatment as God. We expect people to honor and respect us when it's really God they need to honor and respect. If we all honor God the way we say we do, we would automatically respect others. (That's a word for me as well). We are His children so when people disrespect us, abuse us, lie to us, etc., they are doing it to God. Parents, how do you feel when kids or even adults hurt your child? It's like they hurt you right? It's not the same with God and us though, it's even deeper.

We have to move ourselves out of the way, check our feelings and stay in our place. God deserves the honor and glory. We deserve nothing, yet God still gives us everything. Our expectations are only from the Lord and He expects us to love others and treat them with respect. God wants us to look at ourselves lower than others which only means to be humble. So yes, you may think or feel someone should be further ahead spiritually, mentally, or emotionally, but compared to Christ so should you. God tells us we will be judged by the same measure we judge others, so let's take it easy on them, and keep praying for them and ourselves.

Prayer:

Father God,

You deserve the absolute highest praise. Thank You, God, for keeping me even when I don't realize I have sinned against You. Father forgive me for judging Your people and forgive me for thinking of myself higher than I should. Help me to remember that I am to love Your children the way You love me. Help me to also stay humble and focus on myself. Lord show me how I can keep growing in my relationship with You. I confess that I will no longer be distracted by other people's choices in Jesus' name. You are the creator of everything, even time so there is nothing You cannot do. I give You my concerns and worries that keep me looking at everything but myself and trust that however You perfect my concerns I will be more than okay. Thank You, Jesus, for sacrificing Your life for me.

In Jesus name, Amen and Amen.

Scriptures

Proverbs 16:18, NKJV
Pride goes before destruction, And a haughty spirit before stumbling.

Proverbs 11:2, NASB
When pride comes, then comes dishonor, But with the humble there is wisdom.

James 4:6, NASB
But He gives a greater grace. Therefore it says, "God is opposed to the proud, but gives grace to the humble."

15

More Than a Wife

Before getting married my only expectations of being a wife were of the basics: getting a ring and his last name, that he would HAVE to be committed to me, that we were able to finally have sex without sinning, and I would have the title "WIFE." Of course, the vows as well, but that was all I knew. After being a wife for about 5 years I can look back and see I was ignorant to rush into something like this. Marriage is beautiful but there is a level of commitment T.V., and people don't really display. I found out God was calling me to be more than a wife to my husband.

Our relationship was never perfect, or even decent for that matter, so I thought if I mastered my role somehow my husband would get on board and we would live happily ever after. Having his kids and even saying "I do" did not change anything in our relationship, and I became even more angry with him and our marriage more dysfunctional. Me trying to be a good wife to him got me results that only lasted for so long then it went back like nothing happened. The frustrations of constantly offering myself and getting less in return continued to break me. God had to explain to me that being a Christian and a wife is not a trade. I am not to expect anything in return from man but only God. He is the rewarder. As Christians we do not forgive others, respect others, and do for others just so we can put them in debt. We don't do those things because that person is EXPECTED to give back what we gave them. We do them because we have God's heart and are obedient to Him.

After complaining, whining and crying to God, He told me that He needed me to "help" my husband. For some reason, this instruction brought up a lot of negative feelings I had toward his parents. I wanted to help in a simpler way. I wanted to help in ways I knew I signed up for like financially, with the kids, or supporting him in ways that I wanted to if I'm being honest. I became particularly angry at his mother because I felt like all that I was going through was her fault. I felt like I was paying for her mistakes double time. For one, whatever I thought he had against her I was paying for and two, everything that wasn't taught by her I had to teach him. I did not want to be his mother, I wanted to be his wife. (Side note: On the flip side, I also gave my husband a hard time because of where my father has failed in raising me). BUT God! The Lord told me that He needed me to be Deborah.

In the Bible there's a story about a woman named Deborah who led a man named Barak into war because he refused to go without her. As honored as I should have been because God believed in me, I didn't want to lead my husband. You know God *always* uses people who say yes to Him, right? We get frustrated when our spouse isn't walking side by side with us or even where we think they should be. Like me, I wanted my husband to do what I THOUGHT he should have been doing as a leader. I actually wanted to be under my husband, but did he say yes to what I said yes to? Not yes to believing God but yes to solely living *for* Him. It has nothing to do with the "better" Christian, it's about the *willing* Christian. God uses the willing vessel.

God told me that this was just for a season and He showed me several times who my husband was despite what I saw day to day. This was not easy, but I was going to do what the Lord instructed. God sees things in us we don't even see. I have to rest on the fact that He said my husband and I were not going to be in this position forever. God began to show me things about myself that I needed to change to help Him deliver my husband. When I belittle my husband and spoke death I was teaming up with the enemy and coming against my own marriage. If you haven't guessed I was not thrilled about this one either. In my eyes God was being unfair. I already changed to be nicer, I agreed to take temporary leadership and now He wants me to make more changes? I constantly thought about how my husband hadn't even made any real changes for me.

God spoke to me again! He said being a wife is an actual ministry. It means being selfless, flexible, and doing everything with grace and love. I had to be Christ-like. If God tells us to truly love others, including our enemies, we for sure have to do it for our spouses. God called me, so I had to suit up again and be on call for whatever God wanted. I had to:

1. Make time for my husband
2. Be nice (no clap backs) even when he wasn't
3. Listen more and talk less
4. Be humble
5. Stop going through his phone, even when I suspect something (**SUPER HARD**)
6. Let him make his own choices and follow up with "I trust you"
7. Serve him (massage him, pamper him, feed him, clean up after, give him space)
8. Consider his thoughts before making decisions
9. Not challenge him!!!!!!

These were just a few things I began to do and every one of those things HURT MY FLESH so much. I absolutely did not check everything off daily, but I honestly tried my best. God then called me to intercede for him. Not just some little prayer, but the works! God told me to:

1. Anoint his clothes every workday
2. Anoint him every night and even his work van
3. Fast for him while he was away (no food, only water; a partial fast)
4. Get up when he does and PRAY over him
5. Pray for him throughout the day

Love is an action and God is showing me how to REALLY love even when it's hard to. I was instructed to do all of this in secret. God told me not to tell my husband about anything I was doing on his behalf, but just to keep praying and covering him so that God can get the glory. It was exhausting to say the least AND I had to keep fighting the spirits of selfishness, pride and doubt. I would have thoughts like, "What if he doesn't change? What if this is pushing him further into sin because spirits are being agitated? Why isn't he covering me?" That last question was the hardest to get over. Why? My entire relationship with him I have fought for this man in the natural. I made a complete fool of myself when we were younger. Willing to fight girls because he was mine (before marriage of course), and willing to be the side chick and wait my turn to be his main. Going out of the way to do things that were demeaning just to prove that I love him. Doing a bunch of dumb stuff that I would never do again. Now God wanted me to fight as a wife in the Spirit and I had no more fight in me. I didn't have any more patience for him because he used it all up. But God reminded me that no matter what comes my way I am still expected to be a woman of God. Even if my husband is not where I would like him to be, I have a choice to choose God and be good to him anyway. We are called to serve our husbands. We are our husband's helpmate whenever they need it. Even when the head isn't in his right position, God is covering us. God is providing for us, and is loving us. Although we don't get these things from our spouse in this hurtful season, God is showing Himself and everything He is to you FIRST. Until our husbands are able to submit to God, we are to win their hearts by being God's hands and feet. You are more than a wife; you are God's willing vessel.

Prayer:

Father,

Hear my cry, O Lord. Being a spouse is more than what I realized, and I am trying my best to please You. Father, I need you to please give me the strength to be everything my spouse needs me to be. Help me to not expect anything from anyone but You. Help me to relearn what it means to be a Christian and solely dependent on You. Thank you, Lord, for being everything I need in every given moment. God, You said in Your word that those who lose their life find it. I trust Your Word, Lord. That even though I feel my needs are being neglected You will perfect everything for my benefit anyway. I am grateful that serving You will always be a win for me even when it doesn't seem as so. I'm thankful that You love me so much even when I fail on purpose or not. Give me the desire and strength to love my spouse the same. I give You all the honor and glory and I pray that Your will be done in our marriage.

In Jesus's name, Amen and Amen!

Scriptures

Proverbs 31:11-12, NKJV
The heart of her husband safely trusts her; So he will have no lack of gain. She does him good and not evil, All the days of her life.

Titus 2:5, NKJV

to be discreet, chaste, homemakers, good, obedient to their own husbands, that the word of God may not be blasphemed.

Genesis 2:21-25, KJV

And the LORD God caused a deep sleep to fall upon Adam, and he slept: and he took one of his ribs, and closed up the flesh instead thereof; And the rib, which the LORD God had taken from man, made he a woman, and brought her unto the man.

And Adam said, This *is* now bone of my bones, and flesh of my flesh: she shall be called Woman, because she was taken out of Man.

Therefore shall a man leave his father and his mother, and shall cleave unto his wife: and they shall be one flesh. And they were both naked, the man and his wife, and were not ashamed.

1 Corinthians 7:14, NKJV

For the unbelieving husband is sanctified by the wife, and the unbelieving wife is sanctified by the husband; otherwise your children would be unclean, but now they are holy.

16

Don't Feel Like Being a Christian

When you are disappointed, angry, depressed, or hurting in any kind of way, and you still manage to look to God for relief, believe me when I say *that is the most powerful decision you can ever make!* God honors that! He wants to be the one to protect you, rescue you, provide for you and be every type of goodness you can think of. He wants you to rely solely on Him. Trust me, God understands exactly how you feel in your exact situation and He knows how much strength it takes to turn to Him when you're tested. It is a huge statement to say, "You got this Lord, I know you will handle this better than I can." Most importantly, that is having FAITH and believing in His strength.

There've been so many times I felt like this Christian walk was not working because I wasn't getting the satisfaction in my flesh. I didn't see what I wanted to see when I wanted to see it. I wanted to see God's vengeance immediately! When people would hurt me, disrespect me, or use me, I would quickly respond in my flesh. I would not even think twice. To be completely honest, I used to enjoy cussing people out and putting someone in their place. I am a type of person who sits back and observes.

I make note of patterns and won't say anything because I would have to process it all first. I need to know for sure how to address you with facts and not speculations. I needed to know that when I came back with the hammer that I was justified. There was a release whenever I lost my cool and I would not regret it because those people got what they deserved in my eyes. Can I be honest and say I still don't really feel bad for the people I came for along the way? I feel bad only because I disappointed God. I know, I know, I'm a work in progress one day I will feel for them.

A lot of us do not realize that what we CANNOT SEE in the physical is much MORE REAL than what we do. What I mean is, what you do, think, and say literally moves something in the spirit realm. I need an entire book to explain this deeper, but this is just a nugget of knowledge. Our spiritual moves are what matters more than our physical ones.

If we fight "people" (in our flesh), by yelling, cussing, manipulating, and destroying stuff it does absolutely nothing but satisfy the flesh. The real issue never gets touched. Praying, having faith in God, praise and worship, fasting, and using the Word of God against the enemy is what produces change. Even when you don't have the strength or desire to do all that, just simply looking to Him is a move for the win in the spiritual realm. The posture of your heart is all God looks at. If I pray in tongues with a negative attitude one day and sit and cry out to God to help me another, I actually did more by just crying, believe it or not. God interprets our grudges even our silent prayers when we are exhausted and have no words or tears left. The Lord misses nothing!

Sometimes I cry silently and think, "God please do something," and believe that He hears me. I feel the burden becomes a little lighter and the more I press into Him with just my heart, the less stress or agony I feel in the moment of despair. I have experienced God the *most* when I did the *least*. I used to think that if I didn't pray a structured prayer, if I didn't speak in tongues, if I didn't read an entire chapter in the Bible when I was at my lowest, that I wasn't being a good servant and that I was hindering my blessings, but that's a lie. That is the trick of the enemy. God wants intimacy and knows we have feelings. After all, we aren't robots. There will be days when you have the energy to read straight through the Bible and then there are days when you can only read part of a scripture. As long as it ministers. If you hold onto His Word and are truly relying on Him, then you're good. It is something that has to be intentional. He wants to be a part of your life and desires to be a part of you.

It's easy to snap, to throw in the towel, to eat, to have sex, to watch porn, to drink or turn to whatever gives you temporary release, but it is not going to give you true healing and deliverance. Even though you don't feel like being a Christian, I encourage you to just sit in His presence. Vent to Him or be silent. In these moments you'll begin to understand what God means when He says to be still. Being still means, "I'm not going to do it my way Lord." Trying to satisfy ourselves would only delay our promises and make things worse. Not only that, but we also miss the goodness of who our God really is in our hardest moments. We miss the most tender moments of being in the wilderness with Him. God just showed me it's like Adam and Eve hiding from God when they messed up. God wants us naked, transparent, and real with Him. That is true intimacy, that's when we become free. The feeling of being uncomfortable with God will fade the more you do it.

If you're married it's like being physically naked in front of your spouse for the very first time. The more you do it, the more comfortable you become … Maybe that wasn't the best example. What I'm saying is it's like anything else that was new to you. New things always feel different and uncomfortable at first until it's not new anymore. If this is new for you then it's something to be excited about. Keep pressing past the awkwardness and I promise your life will never be the same. Turning to God when I didn't feel like it produced so much growth in my spirit, I can't even articulate it into words. I can only guarantee that you won't be let down when you choose to be a Christian even when you don't feel like it.

Prayer:

Father, in the name of Jesus,

I repent of relying on my own strength and not You. Father only YOU can rescue me out of this situation! And I pray that You give me the strength to come to You when I am angry, hurt, confused. Lord, I give You full control over my situation and even my life. Help me to believe that You are working things out for me.

In Jesus mighty name, Amen.

Scriptures

Romans 8:26, NIV
In the same way, the Spirit helps us in our weakness. We do not know what we ought to pray for, but the Spirit himself intercedes for us through wordless groans.

1 Samuel 16:7, NIV
But the Lord said to Samuel, "Do not consider his appearance or his height, for I have rejected him. The Lord does not look at the things people look at. People look at the outward appearance, but the Lord looks at the heart."

Ephesians 6:12, NIV
For our struggle is not against flesh and blood, but against the rulers, against the authorities, against the powers of this dark world and against the spiritual forces of evil in the heavenly realms.

17

Accepting Double-Minded People

Having a double mind means having a double heart, a double tongue, and a double lifestyle. In other words, fake, fake, fake and fake. I needed to understand why people were able to lie so easily and still live with themselves. Not that I have never lied. I needed to understand how someone could constantly lie and live with themselves.

Double-minded people need to do what they need to do to protect themselves. Anyway, what doesn't make them look bad will be what they choose every time, regardless of how it affects you. People with a double mind operate in witchcraft because it is a way to control what you see, hear, and or feel about them and others. I dealt with a lot of witchcraft in my life because some people refuse to let go of pride. There are times when I can physically *feel* the tension of that spirit or other spirits around certain people. People carry all kinds of spirits and when you have the Holy Spirit in you demons will manifest because they can't stand light. It may not be super obvious to everyone in the room, but you can just feel it. I would ask myself why I became so angry or irritated with this person for something so small or sometimes nothing. The best way I can try to explain it would be when you look at someone and feel annoyed out of the blue. The person may have not even looked at you. I thought I was crazy when these things would happen because I was about peace and pleasing others, but God showed me it's the spirit(s) behind the face that I was irritated with. The spirit that person would operate in would get me worked up because it was something that needed to be rebuked.

Sometimes we want to help people but it's difficult when people cannot see themselves, or when people don't realize they are being controlled by a spirit. You come from a gentle place and all, but it does not matter if that person cannot see themselves. Trust me, I learned the hard way. Spiritual blindness is REAL and if someone is not rooted in Christ they won't see themselves or be open to suggestions to see who they are.

To me the truth is the truth, whether I like it or not, I ALWAYS keep it 100! Not everyone feels like that though and those are the type of people the enemy feasts on. I suggest you seriously intercede for the people who are spiritually blind. It's a special gift to be able to truly see yourself, to be aware of spirits that you operate in and humble yourself for correction. Being humble is being able to be authentic with yourself because you are authentic with God. There is no justifying your sins and wrongs, only accountability and repentance.

I have operated in witchcraft plenty of times even knowingly. From my experience of having a spirit of pride and a lot of other dark spirits, I remember them refusing to allow me to grow. You will never become victorious always playing the victim, and always lying about how you feel will never allow you to experience God's truth. Putting others down will never allow you to attract true friendship because birds of feather. Always being right will never allow you to learn, and always being in control will never allow God to rule in your life. I had to let it go and humble myself to be in fellowship with God.

When you walk alongside God, He has high expectations of you which means there is a sudden correction. He will correct you because He knows you will receive it. God loves us all, but He invests in those who invest in Him. God's correction of us is why we sometimes feel like people get to do and say whatever they want and get away with it. It's not fair right? I completely agree, but it's an honor not to be able to get away with wrong. We are in a different place with God and it's accepting that the people who seem to get away with everything just aren't there yet. God knows they aren't ready, so if God isn't sweating these people, why are we? We all know that double-minded people are wrong for millions of reasons. Don't worry, God will handle them accordingly. We have to accept that when God is ready to humble someone He will.

God will use the people who hurt us to teach us and help us grow. The pain I have experienced at the hands of others pushed me to God. It's sad it took me being hurt and let down by people to realize how amazing God is but hey, whatever it takes right? I will be forever thankful for my afflictions because of where they have led me, which is straight into the arms of True Love and Security. So even though I was angry at God and others during my trials, I realized I needed people to wrong me because it was proof that ONLY God would be faithful to me. Remember

God uses the enemy's devices for our good. He makes everything purposeful. It can be frustrating dealing with double-minded people, but it's their own struggle to be real with others and themselves. Glory be to God for the double-minded people. We may not see or understand it in the moment, but our experiences with them are a blessing that opens our eyes and blesses us to grow in Him.

Prayer:

Father,

You said a double-minded man is unstable in all of his ways. Father, I repent if I have been double-minded. I pray that You help me to not be controlled and moved by emotions whether it's my situation or people in my life. Help me to have compassion for those who are struggling with double-mindedness. God, whatever is keeping them unstable, I ask that You heal it, Lord. I thank You for changing my perspective so that I can grow spiritually. I give You all the honor and glory.

In Jesus' mighty name, Amen.

Scriptures

James 1:6-8, NKJV
But let him ask in faith, with no doubting, for he who doubts is like a wave of the sea driven and tossed by the wind. For let not that man suppose that he will receive anything from the Lord; he is a double-minded man, unstable in all his ways.

18

In Closing

I would love to tell you that after you decide to surrender your life to God everything will become all smiles and easy but that's not true. Even as I finish this book my heart is heavy. I'm still in a dark place but I know my breakthrough is here and this wilderness season is coming to an end. Even so, I realize that this won't be the last time I visit the wilderness and it may not be the last for you either and that's okay. Establishing a true relationship with the Lord will help you make sense of situations and will release you from drama, stress, anxiety, worry and fear. As crazy as it sounds, when God allows us to experience trouble, we should embrace it. Life is not going to always be easy so instead of complaining and being a victim, be the sunflower and seek His light in your dark place. I assure you, God is there and is shedding His light over you and your situation. Allow God to see you through the struggle so that you are victorious.

It's easier said than done but the beauty in our relationship with the Savior verses man is that the He is patient, understanding, comforting, and on standby in any way we need Him to be. No man on Earth is that dependable. This doesn't mean He will completely remove every challenge we face because it's there to grow us. We have to be willing to grow into a mature sunflower KNOWING and have unwavering confidence that His light is always on us and our situation. We have to believe that we will get through every dark season because He is a good God. What we experience is not for nothing, our wilderness season is not for nothing. Today, choose to be Bare in front of the Lord. Give Him every negative feeling, thought, and situation. He will change your perspective and that is when you will become BOLD and BEAUTIFUL for His Kingdom.

As I continue my journey with the Lord, I will continue to share the revelation He gives me to you. I believe this is only the first Bare, Bold and Beautiful book and there are more to come. With these books I pray that what the Lord speaks to me will bless and encourage you as much as it has for me if not more.

Isaiah 61:1-3, NIV
The Spirit of the Sovereign Lord is on me,
because the Lord has anointed me
to proclaim good news to the poor.
He has sent me to bind up the brokenhearted,
to proclaim freedom for the captives
and release from darkness for the prisoners, to proclaim the
year of the Lord's favor
and the day of vengeance of our God,
to comfort all who mourn,
and provide for those who grieve in Zion—
to bestow on them a crown of beauty
instead of ashes,
the oil of joy
instead of mourning,
and a garment of praise
instead of a spirit of despair.
They will be called oaks of righteousness,
a planting of the Lord
for the display of his splendor.

Made in the USA
Monee, IL
05 June 2021

70329922R10059